#Quote#

"Life has educated me, somebody else's loyalty, cannot be controlled.

Never expect anything in return, don't set yourself up for a fall.

Someone may mean the world to you,

but you may only be an option to them."

Sometimes we care for those too much,
who care very little back?

Because you feel that way,
that doesn't mean they feel that way.

Know the difference between,
people who say they care

and people who actually do care."

#Quote#

"Life educated me; in the proper way;
in the longest way possible.

But I learnt the following very deeply.

There comes a point in your life when you realise who matters and who never did, who won't anymore and who always will.

And in the end, you learn who is fake who is true and who would risk it all for you.

It is only through adversity that we realise who will stand strong with us. It is only when the trials and tests prevail that we learn. We learn who is beside us. Who is standing behind us during conflict? And who is yielding the sword with us."

#Quote#

"When the storm hits, it is then we realise the true aftermath. It is when we pick up the pieces, we realise what we had.

You are strong for getting out of bed in the morning when it feels like hell."

#Quote#

"You are brave for doing things which scare you and make you anxious.

And you are amazing for trying and holding on to what you have when life is hard.

It's only when you are pushed to your limits. You rise further past your expectations.

Sometimes we fall in order to rise."

#Quote#

"The users and abusers.

The only people who get upset when you set boundaries are the ones who benefit from you having none.

Setting boundaries is the love that you set for yourself. This is the key to separating the users from the carers.

Don't focus just rely on the boundaries that are set by you for you."

#Quote#

"Maybe I can't stop the downfall, but I will walk and join you for a walk in the rain.

Those that hold your hand through thick and thin. All the ones that are golden without the need to ask. These are the ones that you should cherish, the ones that come without asking.

The ones that will put their plans to one side. Because they know of the hurt that you are experiencing.

Sometimes we just need someone to listen. And other times we seek advice. Getting this all from one person who cares enough to make space for you.

It is better than having 1000 friends.

You can't put a price on affection."

#Quote#

"The worst distance between people is misunderstanding.

The worst outcome is when you assume to know what the other is thinking.

Misunderstanding and assumption is the mother of all fuck ups in the relationships.

Becoming distant from people who misunderstand you and who assume you."

#Quote#

"Do not be afraid to walk your path of life alone.

The path becomes clearer as the fog of the future clears. So, continue through the mist and uncover what lies ahead.

"It is only through new realisation that we learn the

fundamental concept behind the 'new.'

Walking alone sometimes brings together what you cannot achieve collectively."

#Quote#

"You are put on this planet to do more than, just eat sleep and shit.

You are put on this planet to do more than. Pay bills, bring up children and retire.

You are put on this planet to do more than. Argue and walk alone."

"You are put on this planet to do more than. Get by and except the norm.

You are put on this planet to do more than. To live in boundaries and restrictions.

You are put on this planet to do more than. Be told and be corrected."

"You are put on this planet to do more than. Learn and teach.

You are put on this planet to do more than. Fight or flight.

You are put on this planet to do more than. Relax or prosper

You are put on this planet to do more than. Hurt or be hurt."

"You are put on this planet to do more than. Fall or rise.

You must focus. Focus on what you want to be not what you think you can be."

#Quote#

"Sometimes we have to break before we shine.

Difficult roads lead to better outcomes.

Make a plan and stick to it.

And watch the world turn in your favour."

#Quote#

"There comes a point in your life when you realise who matters and who never did, who won't anymore, and who always will."

"And in the end, you learn who is free, who is true and who would risk it for you."

#Quote#

"The worst distance between two people is assumption and misunderstanding."

#Quote#

"The question is who is going to let me; the question is who is going to stop me."

#Quote#

"Never chase love affection or attention.

If it isn't given freely, then it isn't worth a thing."

#Quote#

"Life is a camera. Just focus on what you want. And capture it into your life.

If something doesn't work out, take another shot."

#Quote#

"They laugh at me because I am not the same.

I understand because they are all the same."

#Quote#

"Her touch tickles me like the cool blanket of the ocean.

My body yearns for the warmth one day, soon."

#Quote#

"Love is tricky, the first time we absorb.

The second time we realise what not to do.

The third time we show what we want.

The fourth time we understand the meaning of love.

The fifth time we realise love is it tool. I'm not an emotion, feeling or desire."

#Quote#

"Life after love.

Stage one – unhappiness emptiness.

Stage two – perception shift.

Stage three – seeking answers and meaning.

Stage four - finding answers.

Stage five – disillusionment of feeling lost.

Stage six, - repairing one within.

Stage seven - joy by loving again."

#Quote#

"If you do not come out of this lot down with a new skill, better knowledge, better health.

You never needed extra time.

You needed discipline."

#Quote#

"Trust in the journey, the journey that you are having.

Understanding the journey is something outside your understanding.

Focus and gain clarity within the steps that you take."

#Quote#

"Resonate with people who are trusted intuitively.

Resonate with like mindedness.

Resonate with connectedness.

Anything else, he's a waste of energy."

#Quote#

"Healers heal nothing.

The ones who heal teach one.

Participating in your own healing is key.

Participating in your own healing through reliance on another. Never."

#Quote#

"Hugging someone brings embrace.

Hugging thoughts of someone brings clarity."

#Quote#

"Loneliness becomes apparent.

Only if the person inside, is unliked.

Make friends within. Only then loneliness transpires not."

#Quote#

"Months of consistent hard work.

Can put somebody years ahead.

Never underestimate the power behind consistency."

#Quote#

"If a mountain seems too big,
start with a hill.

If you feel left behind, it is okay
to slow down.

If you cannot move forward,
move sideways.

Sometimes different perspectives brings out different results."

#Quote#

"It has been a blessing in disguise.

Locked away inside.

The pipeline is empty, and the present moment can be lived.

Think of the positive in every situation.

And positive things will happen."

#Quote#

"Life becomes easier,

When negative people no longer exist in one's life.

Turn your radar on, that's what is therefore?

Listen to the good feeling."

#Quote#

"Pay attention to the lessons of life.

Reading between the lines is key.

If you cannot, then the lesson must be learnt in a different way."

#Quote#

"Talk less and act more.

Say not show more.

Forget promises, demonstrate."

#Quote#

"Perfection is not needed in a relationship.

Good energy, originality, and priority above all.

And the relationship flourishes'"

#Quote#

"When trust is broken.

Everything is lost.

Trust cannot be replaced by words or actions.

It is priceless. Never break it."

#Quote#

"Be resilient but not offensive.

Be gentle but not fragile.

Be modest not timorous.

Be delighted but not conceited."

#Quote#

"The end

Becomes

A new beginning.

Life is a circle.

Remember."

#Quote#

"Leaving a situation(s). Is ok.

It is better than staying somewhere where you are not valued or appreciated."

#Quote#

"A woman's worth is leading her man.

A man's worth is protecting her to walk the earth freely."

#Quote#

"The mind is not a recycling bin.

Keeping hatred jealousy and anger; fills the mind with rubbish thoughts of negativity and nothing else.

The mind is a treasure."

"Fill it with sweet memories happiness and love."

#Quote#

"Moving forward sometimes feels like a lonely road.

We are simply shredding past energies who no longer serve us.

Those who resonate with us, are yet to encounter us."

#Quote#

"Forgive the past.

Understand why.

But never forget to remove who hurt you.

Don't be the fool."

#Quote#

"The only difference between a weed and a blooming flower.

Is judgement."

#Quote#

"A person's reaction to any given situation.

Has the power to change the situation avertedly."

#Quote#

"Positive thinking is not only about expecting positive things to happen.

It is also excepting things happen for the best."

#Quote#

"My body belongs to my partner who excepts me as a whole.

Who falls in love with my soul?

Who looks beyond what they can see?"

#Quote#

"Think positive and positive things will happen to you.

A positive attitude brings much gratitude."

#Quote#

"Form a habit, by choice of yours of yours only.

Anything else simply won't do.

Habits create destiny."

#Quote#

"Every person should realise.
Before you love anyone.

The love must start within.

Dreams of fairy tales transpired
because of self-love."

#Quote#

"Meet me where that game begins.

Become my world. As my world will become yours.

Until then I wait patiently."

#Quote#

"Knock, knock,

Who is there?

Opportunity.

Don't be silly...

Opportunity never knocks twice." (unknown).

#Quote#

"Health is wealth.

We know no knowledge of the value of it,

We know not, until it is lost."

#Quote#

"Your value doesn't decrease.

Based on somebody else's inability to see your worth."

(unknown).

#Quote#

"You are borrowed.

Everything is returned in the end.

Even you will be returned."

#Quote#

"Sometimes we need to walk alone. Only then we can figure out where we need to be. And who we need to be with."

#Quote#

"Sometimes the loneliness brings people who resonate to us."

#Quote#

"What do you want from others.

First become yourself.

Loyalty love and happiness. Can't be found by somebody who cannot show it to themselves first."

#Quote#

"The mind is where we reside. It is a place of sanctity. It is the temple within.

Make sure it is clean. Only you can do this."

#Quote#

"Life is brief, live it.

Love is rare, attract it.

Anger is wicked, scrap it.

Fear is unpleasant, face it.

Memories are memorable, treasure them,"

#Quote#

"There is no battle as a flower blooms.

There is no skirmish as water flows.

There is no scuffle for the sun to shine."

"There is no tussle for the grass to grow.

For it is a natural to think otherwise.

Try and learn from nature.

Go with the flow."

(unknown).

#Quote#

"It all started with a friend's request.

Every happily ever after.

Having the freedom, use it."

#Quote#

"The only people who are upset after boundaries are set.

Are the ones who benefited during no boundaries."

#Quote#

"I mean never stop the downfall.

But I will hold your hand and take you for a walk in the rain."

(unknown),

#Quote#

"You and I exist.

We are meant to find each other.

As this is the game of love."

#Quote#

"Make a choice today.

Live to work.

Or work to live."

#Quote#

"Immature people win arguments at any cost.

Mature people understand it's better to lose an argument when the cost is too high."

#Quote#

"Don't worry about people who talk behind your back.

They are behind for a reason."

(unknown).

#Quote#

"The worst regret we have in life, it's not for the wrong things we did.

As there is forgiveness for that.

It is the countless things we did, for the wrong people."

(unknown).

#Quote#

"What you can't say owns you.

What you hide controls you.

(unknown)."

#Quote#

"When you cannot change the situation or an outcome.

Change yourself."

#Quote#

"When there is no trust in a unity of marriage.

It is like a computer, which cannot connect to the Internet.

Gameplay is all you have."

#Quote#

"Everything you ever wanted.

Is on the other side of fear."

(unknown).

#Quote#

"You could never build a kingdom with somebody who is still craves attention from the village."

(unknown).

#Quote#

"Moments of patience in a discussion.

Can save many moments of regret."

#Quote#

"Know the value of the moment.

Don't wait until it becomes a memory or worse, a regret."

#Quote#

"At any given moment,

You have the power to say:

This is not how my story ends."

(unknown).

#Quote#

"Suffering with who you love is not an easy thing to do.

However, staying with somebody because you fear of them suffering without you:

It is pity not love."

#Quote#

"The definition of insanity is doing the same thing repeatedly; and trying to ascertain a different result.

You do some think the same and expect a different result.

Different perspectives, lead to different results."

#Quote#

"Forget not,

Who help during those difficult times. Who left in your difficult time. And who put you there."

#Quote#

"Things happen for a reason.

Life is a blessing,

For now, smile at the troubles.

Laugh at the muddle of life experiences.

As it all will work itself out in the end."

#Quote#

"Some come into our lives for a reason.

Some come into our lives only for a season.

But both are lessons."

#Quote#

"Unfortunately, it is difficult to tell who is praying for us and who is playing with us.

Only time will tell.

Listen to your gut feeling."

#Quote#

"Sometimes bad situations, bring us to the realisation of something that we may not have been paying attention to."

#Quote#

"No one is ever too busy.

It's always a matter of priorities."

#Quote#

"Never make somebody a priority, who only sees you as an option."

#Quote#

"One day you're important in somebody else's life.

and

One day you are worthless to the same person.

Choose wisely."

#Quote#

"Conditionally,

Or,

Unconditionally,

Your choice, choose wisely."

#Quote#

"Think how difficult it is to change yourself.

Now you understand.

How difficult it is to change others."

#Quote#

"The sanctity of a real love.

They will forgive easily.

Communication becomes key.

Losing you is something they cannot think about."

#Quote#

"You know how much someone faithfully loves you when they unreservedly say it and noticeably show it."

#Quote#

"Friendship means,

Understanding not agreeing.

It means forgiveness not forgetting.

It means the memories last, even if contact is lost."

(unknown),

#Quote#

"Sometimes we need to destroy the bridge behind.

Just in case we change your mind."

#Quote#

"You've got to look for the good in the bad.

The happiness in your sadness.

The gain in your pain.

And what makes you grateful not hateful."

(unknown).

#Quote#

"Not everyone will appreciate what you do for them.

You must figure out, who is worth your kindness and who is taking the piss."

#Quote#

"If you can do something about the situation.

Then why worry.

If you can't do something about the situation.

Then why worry."

(unknown).

#Quote#

"Never think too much,
Never wonder too much,
Never imagined too much,
Never obsess too much,

Have faith in your ability to work things out."

#Quote#

"Stop re-reading your last chapter of your life.

Turn the page.

And let the next chapter begin."

#Quote#

"The choice is yours.

Take a chance.

And change your life forever.

Take a deep breath and just do it."

#Quote#

"10 years from today.

Look back at something you choose.

And not something you settle for."

#Quote#

"Success has two meanings.

The first, success sucks.

Learn the first meaning and then the second meaning will manifest automatically into your life."

#Quote#

"Success is not something that you wait for.

It is something to be achieved.

It is something you go and get it.

Are you ready?"

#Quote#

"Don't worry if people don't like you.

Most people are struggling to like themselves."

(unknown).

#Quote#

"Divorcees,

it is better to be divorced. Then live in a loveless marriage.

Teach your children about love not comfort."

#Quote#

"You're never too old.

It is never too late.

Just remember it is the perfect time for you.

Everything else is inconsequential."

#Quote#

"Open the tap to your success.

And let it pour down with the wealth that you deserve."

#Quote#

"Live the life that you choose to live.

Everything is possible;

It's until we try, we never know."

#Quote#

"Be happy in the skin you are in.

For everybody else is taken."

#Quote#

"Sometimes we get lost for so long that we forget what it was like to be ourselves.

Connect with yourself once again.

Feel the bliss locked away deep inside."

#Quote#

"Sometimes what your in search for comes when you are not searching."

#Quote#

"You could meet somebody tomorrow who may better suit you.

More that a person that knows, you too well."

#Quote#

"Trust your gut feeling.

If something is not right with a situation or person.

Trust it."

#Quote#

"Create a space in your mind.

By giving up what no longer serves you."

#Quote#

"To find peace.

Stop your mind traffic.

Stop the noise created by people places and things."

#Quote#

"A person needs a partner with real attentions.

Not a partner who can't pay attention."

#Quote#

"Stop going to those who ignore you.

Start going to those who adore you."

#Quote#

"A lot of partners say good partners do not exist.

A lot of partners don't know good Partners when they experience it."

#Quote#

"The partners with the tallest wall have the deepest love.

Climb the wall and see."

(unknown).

#Quote#

"Never miss use someone who loves you.

Never focus on busyness, over someone who need you.

Never cheat trust.

Forget not the one who remembers you the most."
(unknown).

#Quote#

"Find the good in people.

And ignore the bad in them.

Not many are perfect."

#Quote#

"Start a new relationship.

With the person who creates you.

Not controls you."

#Quote#

"Plenty of partners want to hook up.

And share nothing.

The right ones.

Share everything."

#Quote#

"Showing your good side brings everybody.

However,

Showing your bad side, brings some body's."

#Quote#

"There is no such thing.

As a.

Part-time partner."

#Quote#

"You never appreciate what you have until it is gone.

You also appreciate the peace."

#Quote#

"As one door closes.

Sometimes it is best to wait a while before opening the next door.

Healing is key.

Everybody heals at a different pace."

#Quote#

"Defeat is merely time to start again.

And rebuild and strengthen one's foundations.

For triumph."

#Quote#

"One can be the purest form of entity.

But you still have to modify your character.

And adjust your behaviour."

#Quote#

"Less control.

More freedom.

It is all about trust."

#Quote#

"People who look for faults in others.

Look past faults of their own."

#Quote#

"Your mind can play trickeries on you.

Your heart can lead you a stray.

Your beacon of truth signals within your gut."

#Quote#

"Letting people finish their conversations.

Sometimes it is better to be ignorant.

Then listen to Twaddle.

Stand guard at your minds gate"

#Quote#

"Observe.

Not.

Absorb."

#Quote#

"Detox your life.

Liars welcome not.

Disrespecting need not apply.

Uses walk away.

Resonating starts with you."

#Quote#

"Rich people live under their means and stay rich.

Others live outside their means and have no riches."

#Quote#

"There is no such thing as a lonely heart.

There is merely the heart which is ready to be filled."

#Quote#

"You are going to feel pain.

Regret.

Or.

Growth."

#Quote#

"People love materialism.

People like people.

Truth be told.

People love people.

People like materialism."

#Quote#

"People will teach you how to love.

By loving you not."

(unknown).

#Quote#

"Societies will teach you how to forgive.

By apologising not."

(unknown).

#Quote#

"Folks teach you kindness.

By their judgement."

(unknown).

#Quote#

"Individuals that teach you how to grow.

By stagnant."

(unknown).

#Quote#

"I don't care if you don't like me.

I really like me."

#Quote#

"We are spiritual beings having a human experience.

Experience life without trying."

#Quote#

"Courtship begins by training.

Chivalry begins by earning.

Engagement begins by engaging."

#Quote#

"Go further than you have ever been.

That's growth."

#Quote#

"Go somewhere different each year.

Open your mind to new possibilities.

Change your minds perception of life."

#Quote#

"If you weren't happy yesterday.

Try something else today.

Repetitiveness sometimes not needed."

#Quote#

"One day somebody is going to look at you with a light in their eyes that you haven't seen.

They will look at you like you're everything that they've been looking for their entire life.

Wait for it"

(unknown).

#Quote#

"Some people aren't loyal to you.

They are loyal to the need of you.

Once the need changes.

So does their loyalty."

(unknown).

#Quote#

"Showmanship,

Takes after fake-ness.

Be careful who you let into your life."

#Quote#

"Be the beauty of what you perceive to be what you love."

(unknown).

#Quote#

"If being me does not 'wow' you.

Then I'm not your gift to unwrap."

(unknown).

#Quote#

"A person who must destroy others to succeed.

Must realise destruction awaits near his success."

#Quote#

"Overthinking creates problems.

Never solves anything.

Think without thinking."

#Quote#

"Life chapters are there to teach.

Live characters are there to meet.

You must read within intent to reach the end."

#Quote#

"The feeling when somebody genuinely wants to know you.

You can't put a price on that."

#Quote#

"Some people can do the right things.

But yet say all the wrong things.

And some people can say all the right things.

But yet do all the wrong things."

#Quote#

"Sometimes people expect one to be okay with something they are not."

#Quote#

"Never think too hard about the past.

It brings tears.

Don't think more about the future.

It brings fears.

"Live this moment with a smile.

It brings cheers."

(unknown).

#Quote#

"Fuel drama performances.

Need no attendance."

#Quote#

"If one doesn't go after what they want.

They will never have it."

(unknown).

#Quote#

"If one does not ask the answer.

It will always be a 'no'."

(unknown).

#Quote#

"If one does not step forward.

Then the same place becomes a reality."

(unknown).

#Quote#

"I'm not a black sheep.

Everyone else is blue."

#Quote#

'Marry a lazy person.

Every day is labour day."

#Quote#

"Behind every strong person.

There is a person who wronged them somewhat."

#Quote#

"Regulations, boundaries, rules and restrictions.

Are for people who colour within the lines."

#Quote#

"Marry a cheater or a liar.

Every day is April Fools' Day."

#Quote#

"Be soft do not let the world make you hard.

Do not let the pain make you hate.

"Don't let the bitterness take away your sweetness."

(unknown).

#Quote#

"People who are claiming to be never wrong.

And make you feel like it's your fault.

Distance behind is better."

#Quote#

"Not everyone under the mask of friendship.

Is your friend."

#Quote#

"Whatever you say in a relationship.

Can be used against you.

Sync your knowledge slowly."

#Quote#

"Making a single friend who stands by you against many.

It is better than making many Friends who are never there."

#Quote#

"Be strong enough to stand alone.

Smart enough to know when you need help.

And, brave enough to ask for it."

(unknown).

#Quote#

"Know which sound system to listen to.

And how to listen to it."

#Quote#

"Your feet are your roots.

Plant them down firmly.

And move slowly and carefully."

#Quote#

"If you don't call me, I'll understand.

If you don't text me, I'll understand.

If I forget you, you'll understand."

(unknown).

#Quote#

"Be a good person, forgive intently.

But trust is lost."

#Quote#

"Time is like a river flowing.

One cannot touch the same water twice."

(unknown).

#Quote#

"You are calling.

It is something that you're passionate about.

Look into this."

#Quote#

"Truth, honesty, love, trust and respect.

Never leave home without them."

#Quote#

"Spontaneous is the key to life.

Let it happen when it happens."

The End

Printed in Poland
by Amazon Fulfillment
Poland Sp. z o.o., Wrocław